All Kinds of Jobs

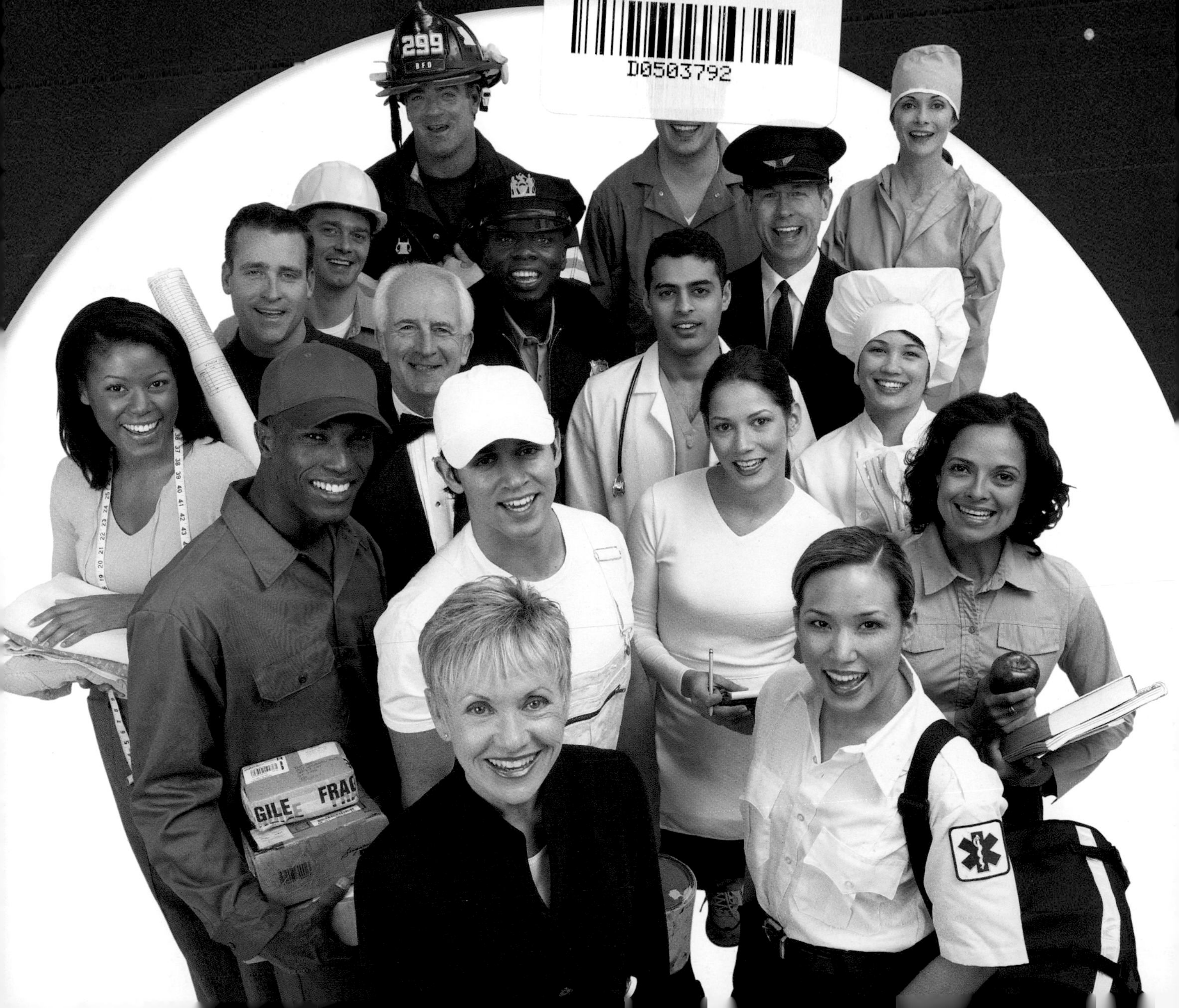

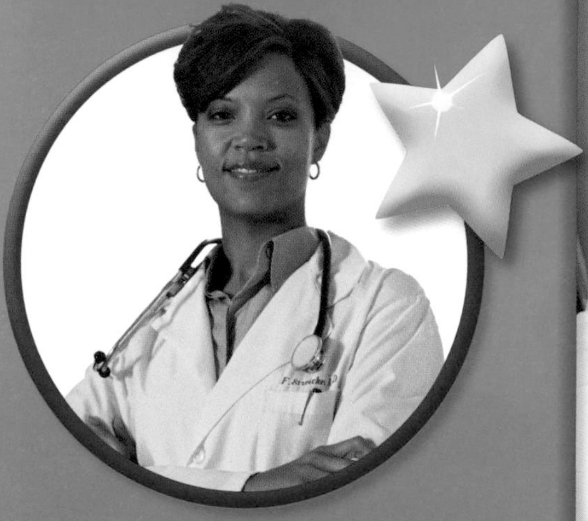
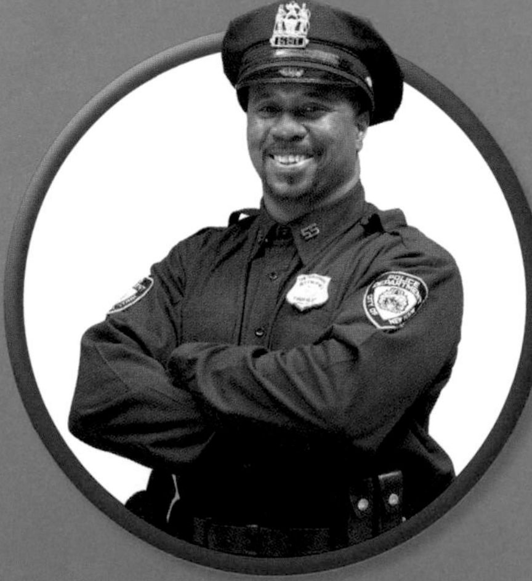
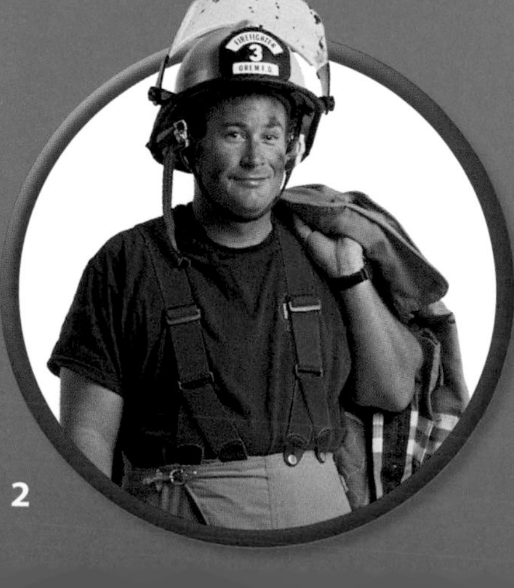
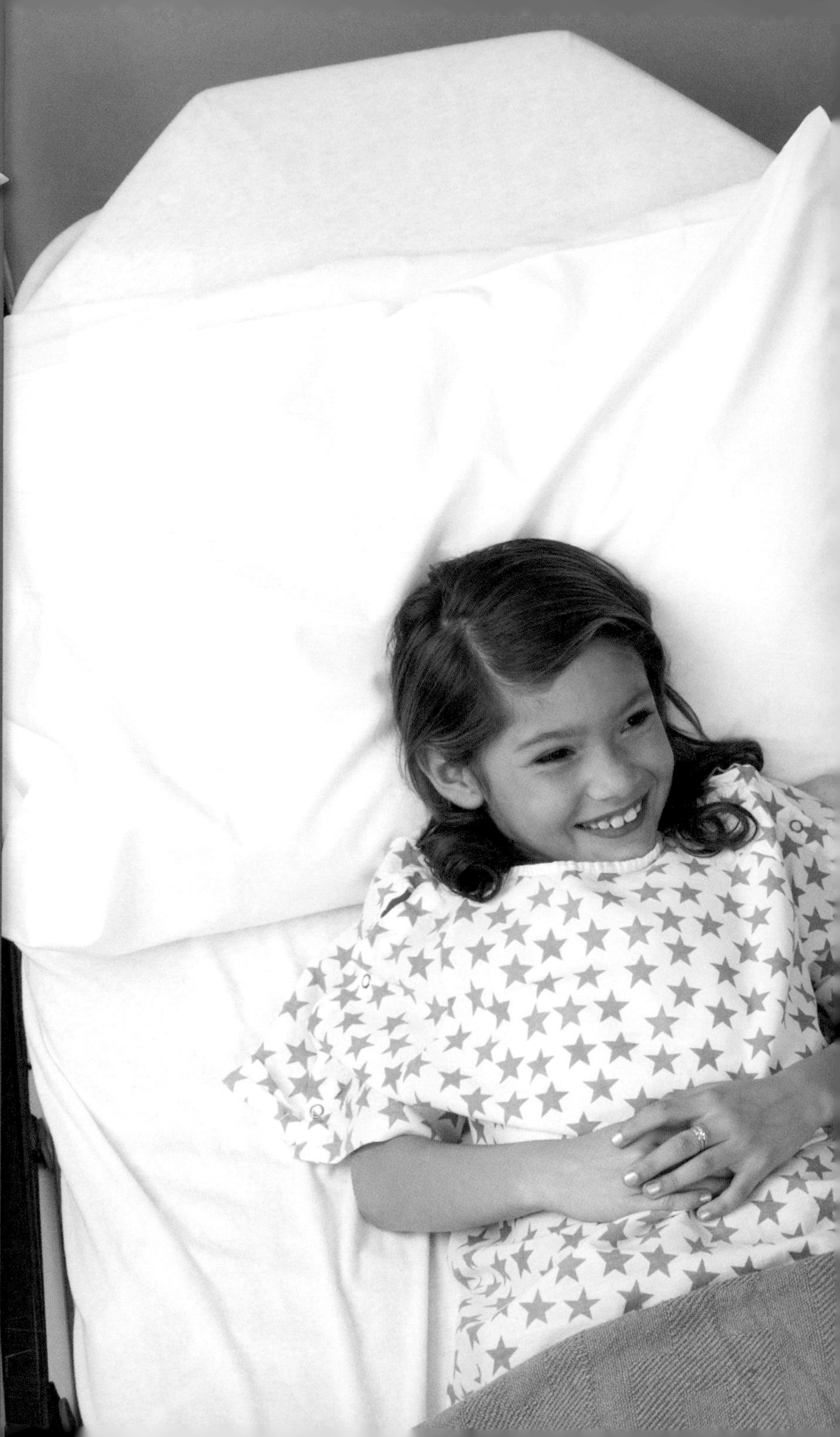

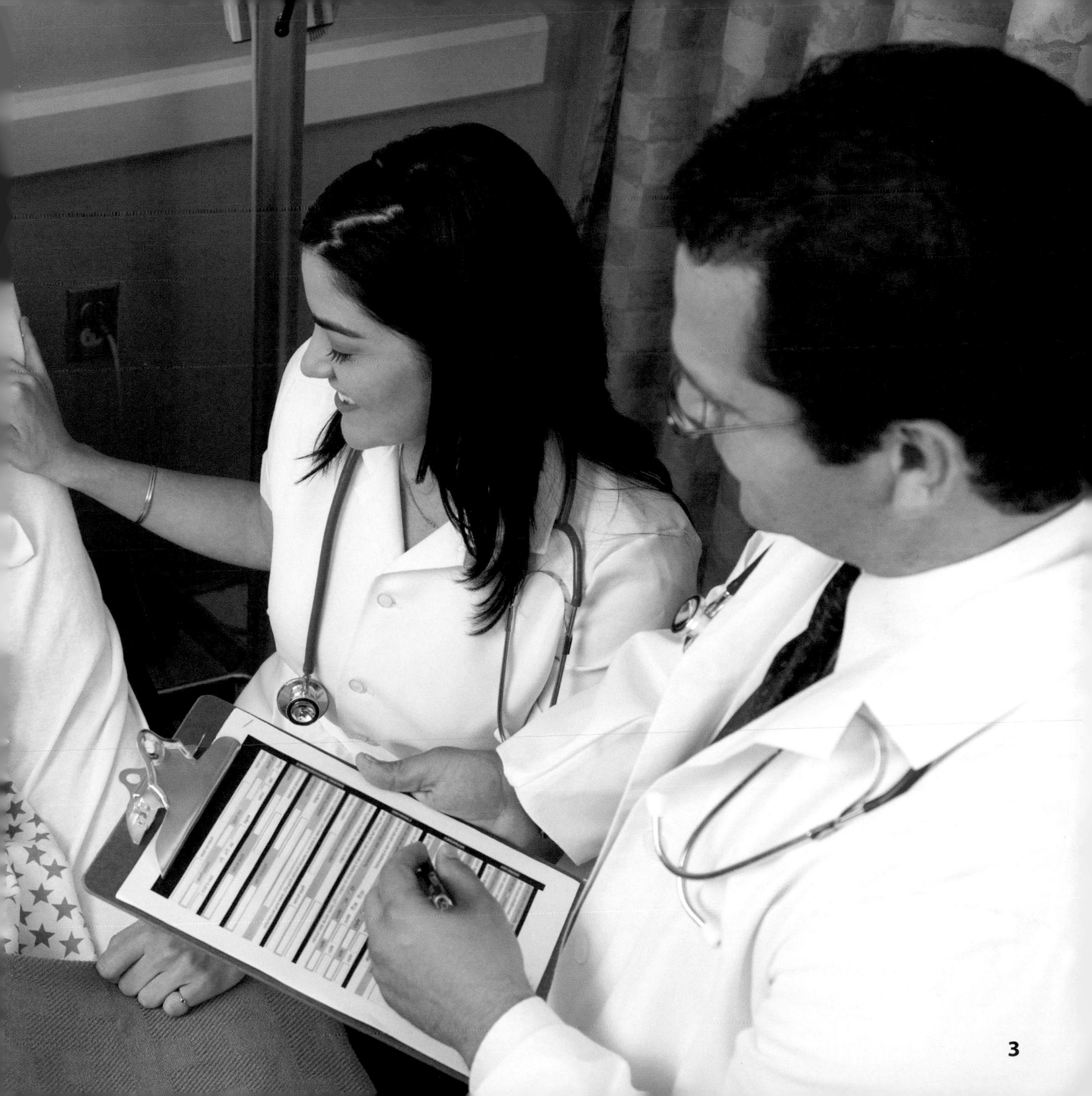

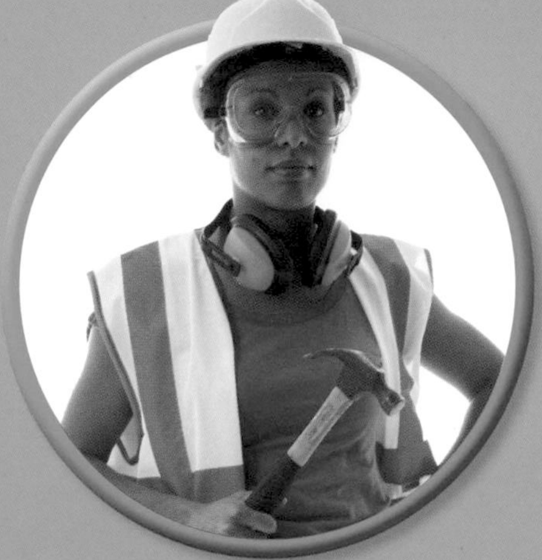

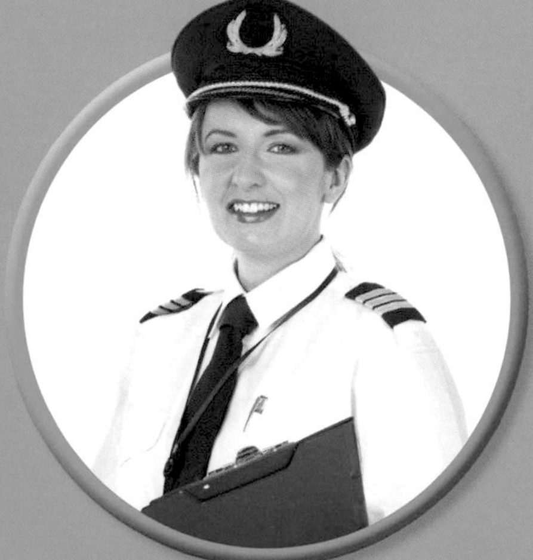

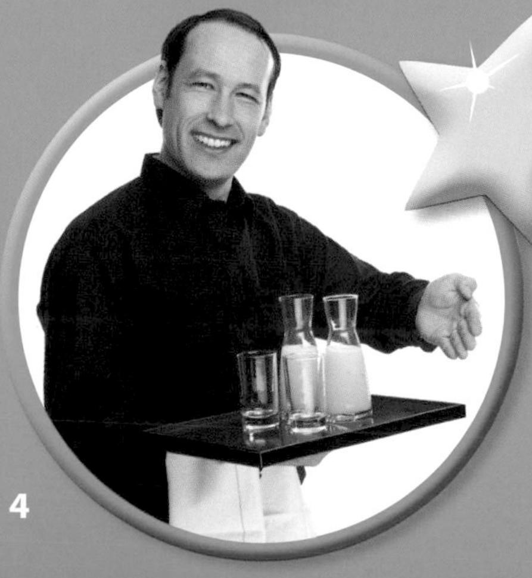

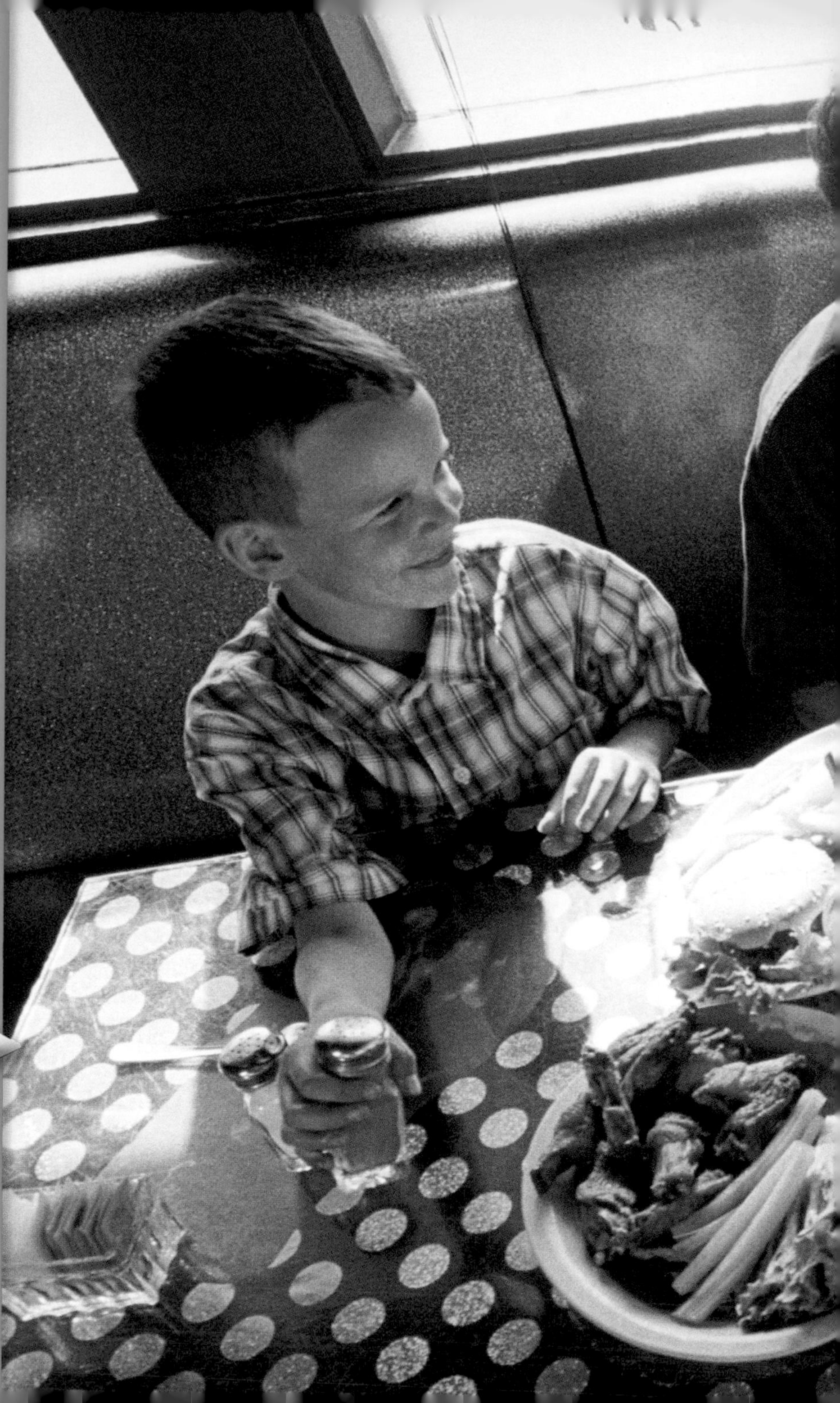

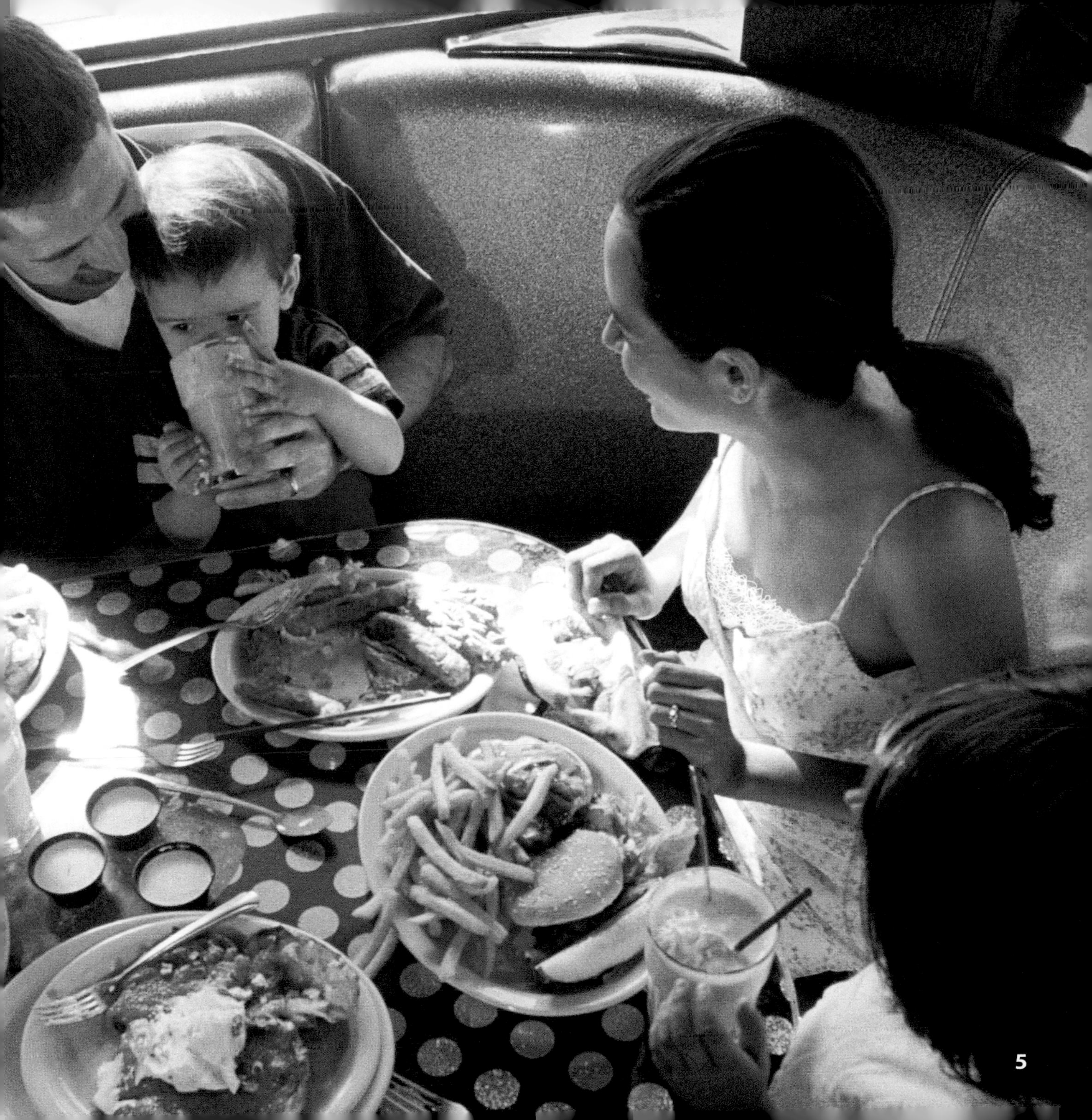

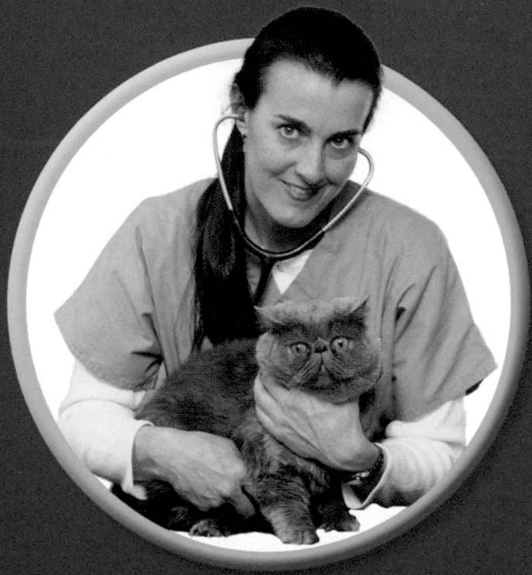
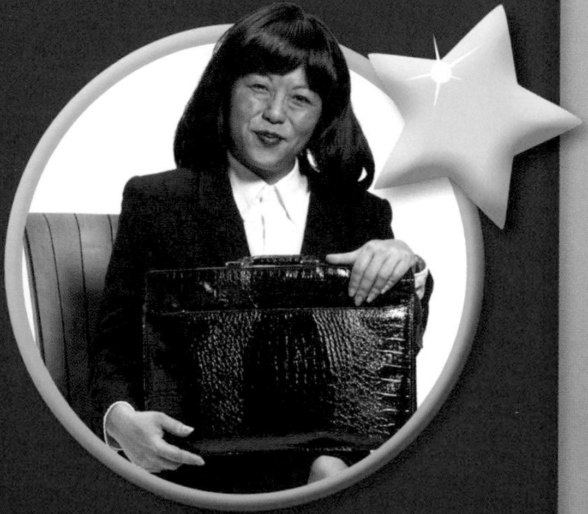
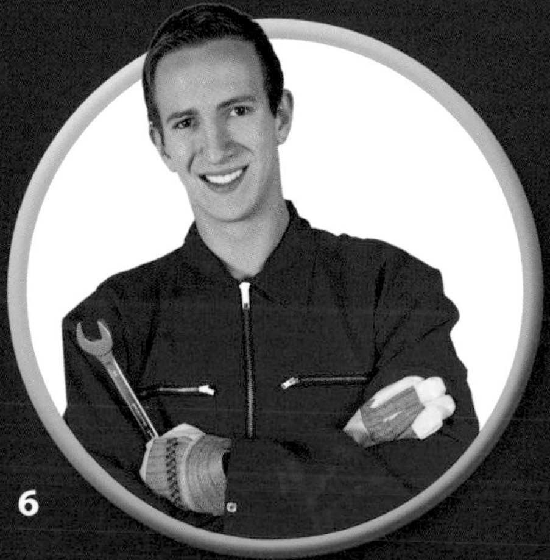
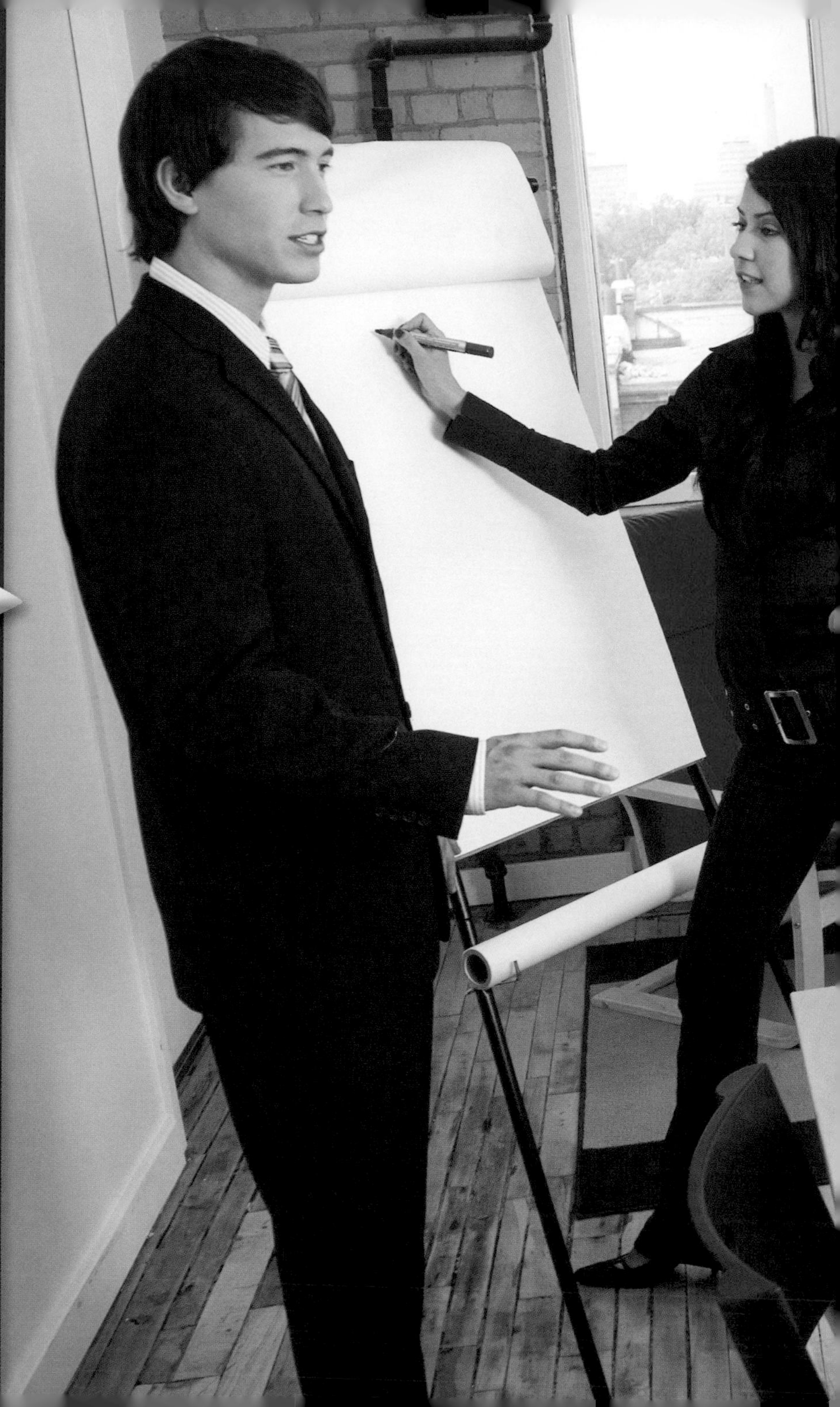

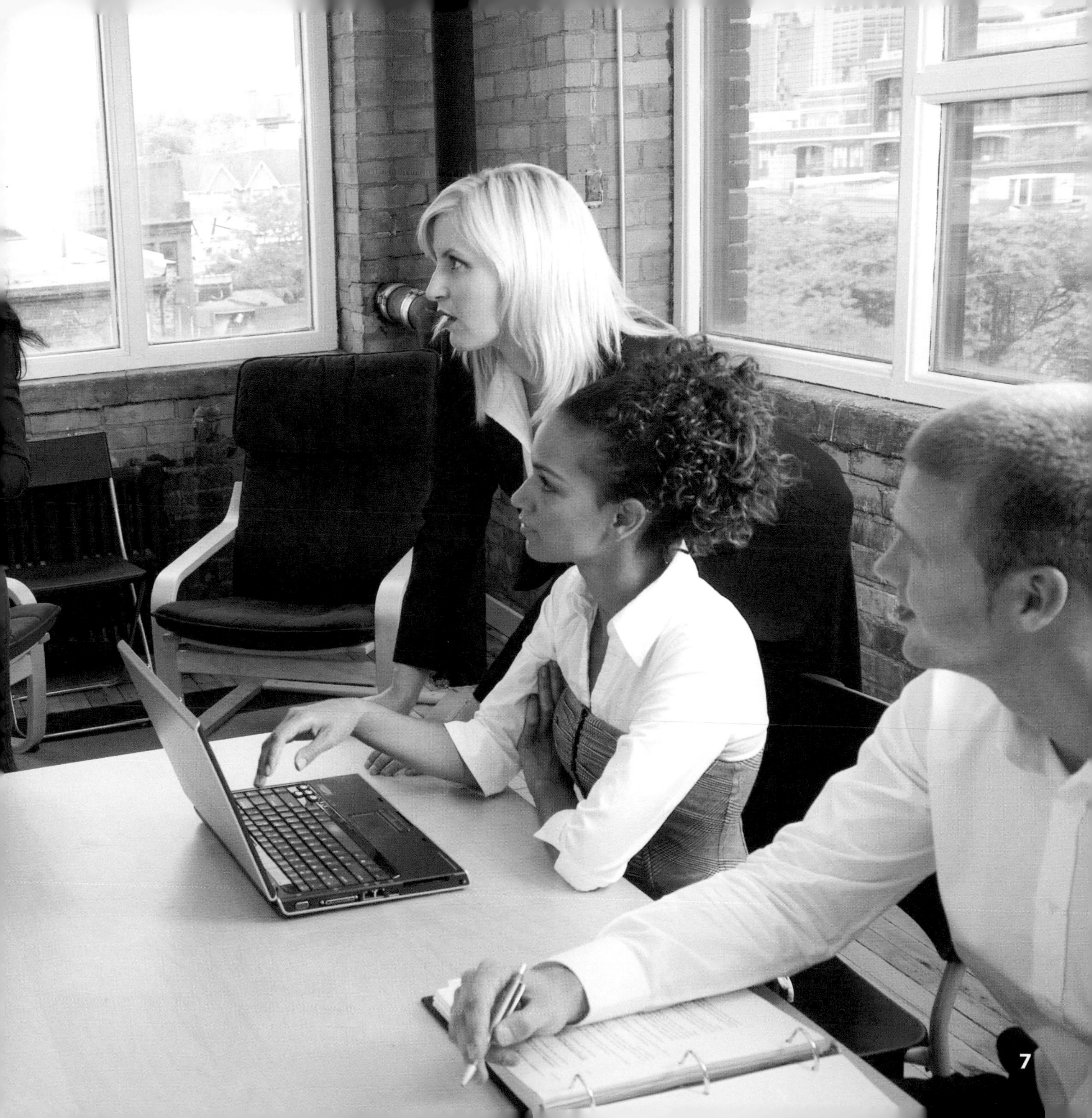

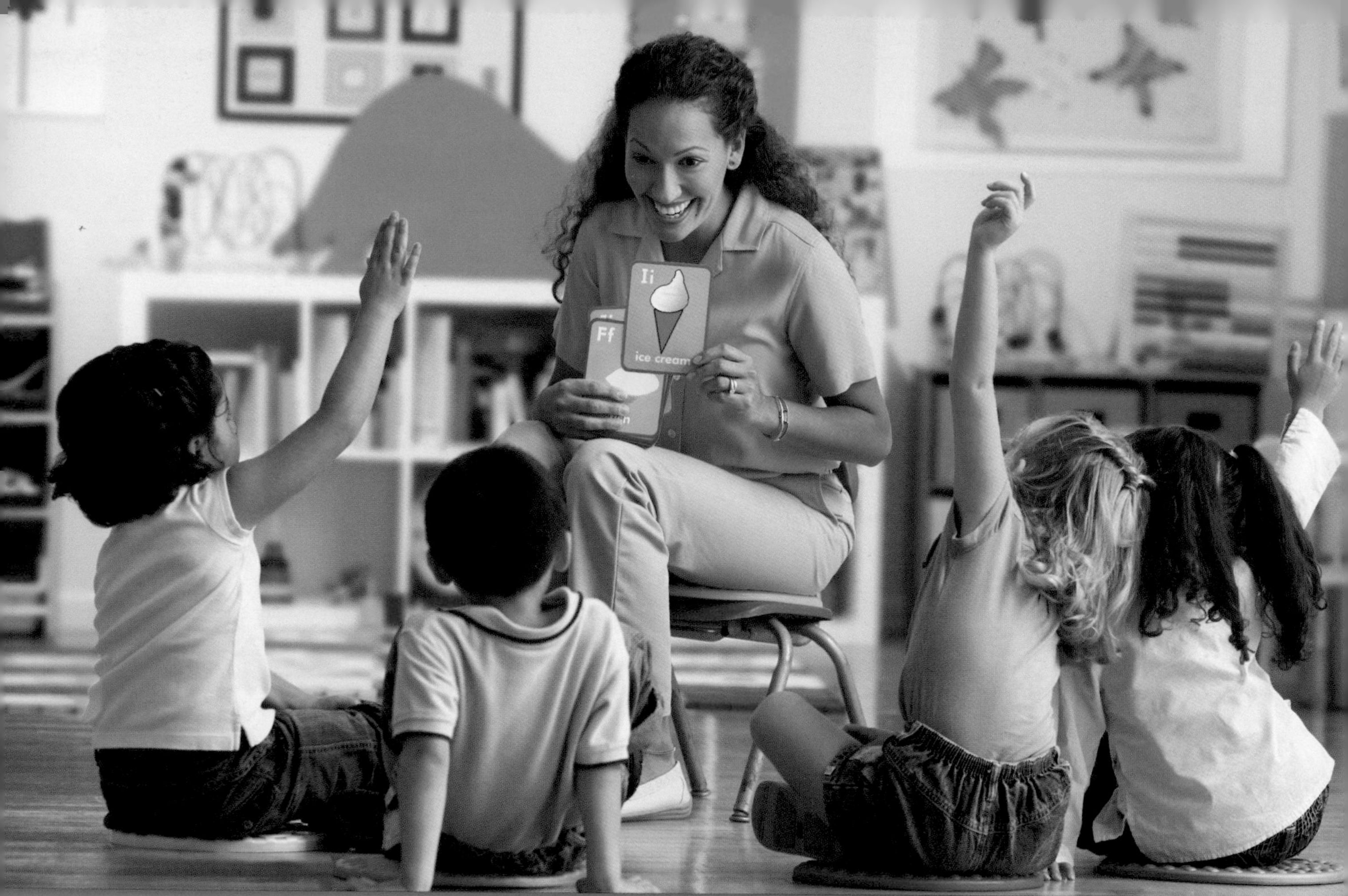

Ii
ice cream
Ff

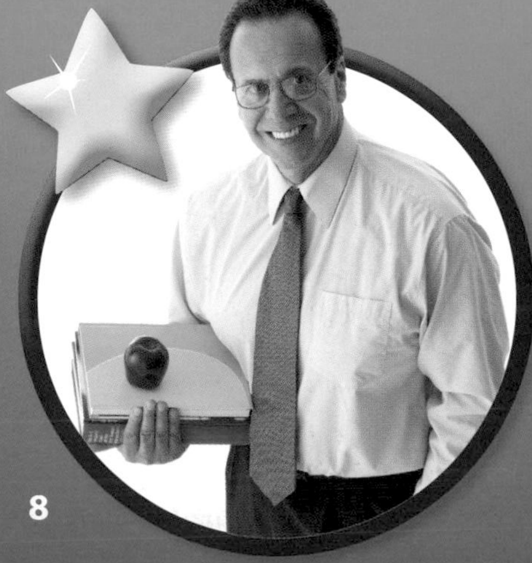

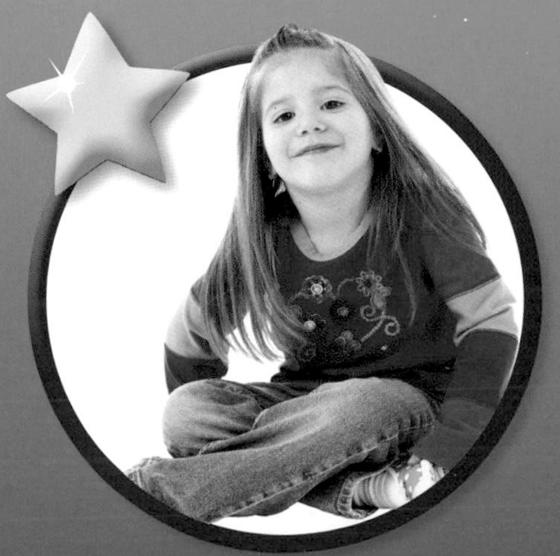

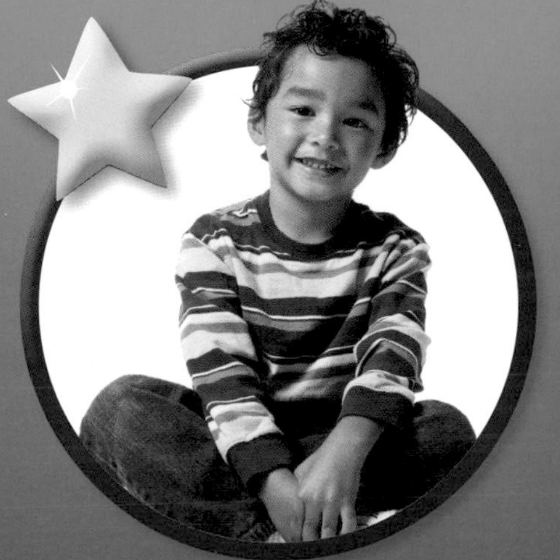